Table of Contents

Introduction

"The matrix is this philosophical idea that the universe, and everything that it's made up of, is a simulation.

Neo: This... this isn't real?

Morpheus: What is real? How do you define real? If you're talking about what you can feel, what you can smell, taste and see, then real is simply electrical signals interpreted by your brain.

... Given how advanced our technology has evolved in the past couple of decades, and how more integrated AI technology has been in our everyday lives... creating a simulation of our world... isn't entirely unlikely.

... technology that can read our movements and virtually replicate them in a simulation is already being developed.[1]

"... Could everything we see, everything we experience, everything that exists in our entire universe be artificial?

supporters of simulation theory believe that not only is it possible that we're living in a simulation,

---

[1] "We're in the Matrix" Tech CEO's Cryptic Last Words. https://youtu.be/oMmoMZzsAVE

... it's likely.

And the more we look for evidence the more we find

... Max Tegmark a cosmologist at MIT said the strict laws of physics point to the possibility of a simulation

putting a cap on the speed of light sure is a good way to keep your sims from venturing out too far from home

Theoretical physicist James Gates thought simulation theory was crazy then he started studying quarks and electrons he found error correcting code buried deep inside the equations used to describe string theory

... yes computer code computer code strings of bits of ones and zeros

Dr gates has changed his mind about simulation theory

In 2017 a group of scientists at the university of washington proved they can embed computer code into strands of DNA

Everything in nature is math look at the Fibonacci sequence ... we see fibonacci numbers and the golden ratio everywhere:

the number of petals on a flower is usually a Fibonacci number-
lilies have three petals, buttercups have five, chicory has 21, and a
daisy has 34... as trees grow the number of branches they form is a
Fibonacci number

... not just plants, animals too!

The ratio of female to male honeybees in a colony is the golden
ratio 1.618

the human body conforms to the golden ratio too ... even a DNA
molecule measures 34 angstroms long by 21 angstroms wide

Fibonacci numbers and the golden ratio from the spiral of
seashells, to the spiral of a galaxy

and everything in between

Fibonacci numbers are everywhere now some claim this is a
coincidence that humans look for patterns in chaos because that's
what we're programmed to do what what program to do it isn't
that interesting by trying to debunk simulation theory they actually
end up proving it no matter what we study whether it's something
the size of a galaxy or as small as an electron everything in the
universe seems to follow patterns and rules in other words a
program

... if we live in a simulation it would make sense that our reality is rendered [in] the same way [that a video game only processes the part of the game a player is currently 'observing']

... quantum mechanics like the double slit experiment and quantum entanglement only makes sense if there's a program at work [2]

[2] Why Files. https://youtu.be/4wMhXxZ1zNM

A Pixelated Universe

"...not only are you living in a simulation

But it's also generated by a system with which you can contact with your spirit

And actually change the simulation itself... Indeed, hack the universe.

What would you do to change the world?

Well, recent scientific findings have strongly suggested that this is indeed the case.

That we live in a simulation and that we as observers have a demonstrable power that goes beyond this.

We are currently participating in the creation of this reality in which we live.

Wait, what?

Are we really living in a simulation?

Well, that's the conclusion that physicists and cosmologists have come to

And while this idea might have been ridiculed in the past, it's now taken very seriously.

The latest cutting-edge experiments in physics have produced some very strange results.

Results that say that our **universe** is not an objective reality

But it actually emerges from something else that is not physical and far beyond our senses.

... The scientific hypothesis that our world is virtual or like a dream has been explored in depth by many scientists including Dr. Brian Whitworth.

He took ... opposite viewpoints: One being materialism, which says that our universe is entirely physical, self-existing and needs nothing else to explain itself.

And the other being the simulation hypothesis, saying that our universe exists as a virtual construct and depends on processing information that happens outside of spacetime.

Dr. Whitworth looked at all the facts that had been gathered ... after extensive analysis, his conclusion was that the data much more suited the simulation hypothesis.

Now... We are in a computer program...

Scientifically, our universe simply makes more sense when viewed as a virtual construct emerging from consciousness rather than simply "matter exists independently of mind"

.... Almost all scientists agree that our universe began to exist at some point in the distant past.

From the materialist point of view

... The fact that the Big Bang came into existence out of nothing is very difficult to explain.

How could everything come from nothing?

But if we look at the universe as a virtual construction, the Big Bang model works perfectly.

Virtual universes always start with information flowing from a zero state

(There is nothing)

Since they need to be initialized/started first, each time a computer game turns on... a Big Bang is created according to the perspective of the game.

In the virtual world itself creation always comes, at the base of nothing because before it does not start there is no space, or time as defined by the rules of this virtual world.

"A pixelated universe"

Another thing to consider are "quantum bits" (or quantum data).

The fact that light is quantified in photons, electricity in electrons, ... Works better if we live in a virtual construction, because in digital processing, all data must have a "minimum quantity" represented by "bits" (data) or pixels, and our world displays the same properties.

All computer-generated images break down into pixels when examined closely.

And that's what science has found in nature.

Over the past century, physicists have discovered that matter is REALLY quantized, made up of inseparable particles billions of times smaller than an atom.

And as scientists discovered more and more how the world behaves... It became clear that nature is a matrix of computable data.

Space is quantized, time is quantized, energy is quantized

... Everything is made of individual data.

Which means the universe has a limited number of components, which means it has a limited number of states.

Which means it's computable.

If the true nature of the universe is actually digital

... And we actually have quantum data of space and time,

... [this] is totally in line with the hypothesis of the simulation.

Well, in the end ... Do I have superpowers? Can reality be hacked?

Can we reprogram nature and take control of our experience?

Are we, in a sense, already doing it but not realizing it?

"Programming" for argument's sake... is there any solid evidence of computer programming in nature?

... Consider the fact of a maximum speed in nature: The speed of light.

In 2011 scientists showed neutrinos traveling faster than the speed of light. But these findings were retracted when it was discovered that the equipment used was faulty.

<u>Nothing has ever been observed traveling faster than the speed of light.</u>

Nature has a maximum speed... and events happening in a virtual world would also have a maximum speed as they would be **limited by a defined processor.**

There is also the curvature of space by massive objects and the dilation of time from a very high speed. Both phenomena are correlated to the effects of virtual processing loading.

The high concentrations of matter in our universe could constitute a strong demand for computer processing, so much so that massive objects could slow down the space-time computer processor (Similar to how high data demands in a computer would slow down the processor speed).

All digital symbols created by the same program are identical to all others in the same category.

In computing terms, objects are simply instances of a generic category. The fact that all quantum objects are identical in each category (Photons, electrons,...) correlates with a digital equivalent, since in a digital world, any object created by the same code is identical

While the objects we see in our world have individual properties, the quantum data from which they are created are all pressed from identical molds.

The simulation hypothesis proposes that this is the case because each piece of data is created by the same program.

Taken together, all of this could constitute what the courts would call "sufficient evidence". Favoring idealism and the assumption of simulation over materialism.

When the coincidences keep piling up and in combination with the power of explanation This makes for a very powerful and plausible argument. Or even proof.

But even more convincing evidence is provided by the fact that certain phenomena can be easily explained by the hypothesis of simulation... But ... models of materialism have enormous difficulties in explaining [concepts such as] *Non-locality and "Quantum entanglement"*

... For materialism to be true, and for the world to exist independent of the mind, the concept of locality is necessary. This means that for objects to interact with each other, they must be nearby. This is what Albert Einstein believed for most of his life.

... In 1982, physicist Alain Aspect put it together and experimented. The results confirmed that non-locality was in fact real... What Schrodinger had called "entanglement" and which was championed by Bohr but ridiculed by Einstein, *was a fundamental property of nature.*

Instant correspondences **can** be observed between two particles that are separated by an unlimited distance in space.

And that only makes sense if the world is a virtual construct.

In a virtual world, distance does not limit matching, since all points in the simulation are equidistant from the source of the simulation

For example, in a computer game, all points on the screen are at a equal distance from the processor and the same effect can be seen in our world.

If our universe is a simulation projected onto a 3D screen, then its processor should be equidistant from all points in the universe.

Non-locality, one of the biggest problems in physics, is easily solved by the simulation hypothesis.

Space seems an illusion created by virtual construction, but what is even more bizarre than the fact that space is an illusion... Is what quantum physics tells us about matter itself. If I were a character in a video game, but was so advanced that it allowed me to be conscious,

and I started exploring my world in this video game, it would seem to me to be made of real, very real objects, made of really physical things.

So if I started studying like the curious physicist that I am, the properties of this thing, the equations that make things move...

And the equations that give me the math that makes the properties of my world

I'll end up... discovering that all these properties are mathematical.

The mathematical properties that the programmer put into the software, which describes everything.

The server that creates you is not in the same reality as yours, it is outside.

If the computer is non-physical for you, what is physical then?

What is physical to us is our virtual world.

"Waves of potentials"

With these observations, matter does not seem to exist.

The matter seems to be the result of an interaction between the consciousness of the waves of potentials. This has been demonstrated repeatedly in even more precise versions of the double slit experiment from the 1920s until today

... One of the hottest ideas in cosmology is known as the holographic principle.

It is the idea that our 3-dimensional universe emerges from 2-dimensional information; ...in the same way that a hologram produces an image in 3 dimensions from information in 2 dimensions.

The holographic principle tells us something very surprising

it says that our ideas of volume, and in a sense of the world, could be some kind of illusion

First of all, it should be clear that this whole holographic thing is the most [to have] happened in our understanding of space, time, [and] matter, since the invention of quantum mechanics and relativity

Quantum theory in general, and the results of experiments that have been done in this era, have reinforced the holographic principle.

At the end of his life, after spending 28 years searching for a unified field theory based on materialism, Einstein seemed to change his mind about the fundamental nature of the universe.

"I must confess that I have been unable to find an explanation for the atomistic character of nature. Some way must be found to completely escape the space-time continuum, but I have not the faintest idea what sort of elementary concept could be used in such a theory." Albert Einstein - October 1954.

"...the distinction between the past, the present and the future is only an illusion, as tenacious as this illusion would be." Albert Einstein - March 1955."[3]

---

[3] Dr. Incognito. The Simulation Hypothesis Documentary. https://youtu.be/pznWo8f020l

The Universe is Not Real

"... In the 1920s ever since it was discovered that Atomic and subatomic particles exhibit both localized particle-like properties and delocalized wave-like properties physicists have become raveled in a debate about what we can and can't know about the true nature of physical reality

Parmenides one of the greatest of the pre-Socratic thinkers [500 B.C.]

... talked about the nature of reality in which he argues that the world we see is an illusion

[...]

.. recent advancement in the field of Information Theory have shown that information is a fundamental part of the universe

information can be defined as a measure of the uncertainty in a system

in other words it tells us how much we don't know about a particular system

this can include everything from the position and momentum of particles to the properties of black holes in the framework of quantum mechanics information plays a central role

... the act of measuring a quantum system can fundamentally alter its state

this implies that the act of measurement or the acquisition of information is an integral part of the quantum world

moreover recent theories such as the holographic principle suggest that information may *be* the very fabric of space-time itself

this idea posits that the **information in a three-dimensional space can be encoded onto a two-dimensional surface much like a hologram**

this implies that the universe may be fundamentally holographic

with information serving as the basic building blocks of reality ... because information occurs at the macro level and also occurs at the subatomic level, some scientists now argue that information is the **only** candidate for such a building block that can explain its own existence as information generates additional information that needs to be compressed thus generating more information in the process

space-time and matter are all the same they exist one by one out of the same building blocks

information is located not only **on the surface** bounding a specific space but **within** the space itself

... recent advancements in Quantum Computing have shown that information can be encoded **in the state of individual particles**

which can then be manipulated to perform complex calculations

this suggests that the *universe is a kind of quantum computer*

with each particle acting as a bit of information that can be processed

to generate new information

... it's really important to understand we're not seeing reality we're seeing a story that's being created for us

Most of the time the story our brains generate matches the real physical world but not always

Our brains also unconsciously bend our perception of reality to meet our desires or expectations and fills the gaps using our past experiences

If the universe produced brains why can't the universe itself be a giant super brain?

everything that we call real is composed of measurements so tiny that it would be difficult to call them real in themselves

our senses are merely biochemical measuring instruments

that turn ... matter into perceptible things that we can know and understand

they don't reveal reality to us so much as help us to survive

the real information emitted from the universe is interpreted in the brain rather than directly perceived

... three theoretical physicists John Clauser, Anton Zeelinger and Allen Aspect were jointly awarded the 2022 Nobel Prize in physics for a 1972 experiment and many subsequent experiments

showing that the local realism view of the universe is likely to be false   *[things are not real!]*

Their work made clear what quantum mechanics really means:

The scientists findings show that the Universe cannot be locally real as particles lack definite spin up or spin down properties **prior to their observation or measurement**

Therefore the simple act of observing a particle changes its state,

contradicting the rules of local realism

In other words, the universe is real but only when you're looking at it *[oh sh*t]*

the Nobel prize-winning experiment also demonstrated that two particles regardless of distance apart can ... continue to be entangled

... Simulation Theory builds on the argument philosophers have been having for centuries, which is that we can never know if what we're seeing is real

... the question of whether we live in a simulation or not is one that is both captivating and mysterious

it challenges our understanding of the world and ourselves and forces us to confront the limitations of our own knowledge and perception

while the simulation argument is a fascinating concept to ponder it is important to remember that we must approach it with a healthy dose of skepticism and humility as we continue to push the boundaries of technology and explore the frontiers of science we may one day be able to answer the question definitively but until then we must remain open to the possibilities of the unknown

and continue to seek out new insights and perspectives on the world around us

in the meantime we should focus on embracing the reality that we can measure and observe

and resist the temptation to impose our own biases and preconceptions onto the world only by doing so can we hope to gain a deeper understanding of the universe and our place within it so let us keep asking questions keep exploring the mysteries of the world and keep striving to uncover the truth

no matter where it may lead us"[4]

---

[4] Fexl. https://youtu.be/GQpgVWLqo_c

Current Theoretical Physicist James Gates Chats with Neil DeGrasse Tyson on Findings in the Field of Simulation Theory

"JG: When you then try to understand these pictures you find out that buried in them are computer codes just like the type that you find in a browser when you go surf the web and so I'm left with the puzzle of trying to figure out whether I live in the matrix or not"

NDT: wait you're blowing my mind at this moment so you're saying-are you saying your attempt to understand the fundamental operations of nature leads you to a set of equations that are indistinguishable from the equations that drive search engines and browsers on our computers?

JG: that is correct so my -

NDT: Wait, I'm still... what? I have to just be silent for a minute here

... so you're saying as you dig deeper you find computer code rich in the fabric of the cosmos into the equations that we want to use to describe the cosmos?

JG: yes computer code computer code strings of bits of ones and zeros

NDT- it's not just, sort of *resembles* computer code?... you're saying it IS computer code... computer code?!

JG: It's a special kind of computer code that was invented by a scientist named Claude Shannon in the 1940s that's what we find very very deeply inside the equations that occur in string theory and in general and systems that we say are supersymmetric

NDT: time to go home... I think. ... I'm not ... so so are you saying we're all just ... there's some entity that programmed the universe and we're just expressions of their code?

JG: well I didn't say that

NDT: like the matrix ... do you know what you said?

JG... in fact to answer your question more directly, I have in my life come to a very strange place because I never expected that the movie the Matrix might be an accurate representation of the place in which I live"[5]

[5]Hidden Halo, James Gates Shocks Neil DeGrasse Tyson We Live In A Computer Simulation
https://www.youtube.com/watch?v=KSe3rRizzFE

Modern Philosophical View on Simulation Theory

"Professor Robin Hansen has written a modern guide for those who think they are living in a simulation:

... care less about others

... live more for today

... make your world look lively

... become eventually rich

... try to participate in pivotal events

... be entertaining and praiseworthy

... and keep the ... people around you happy and interested in you

it's that simple ... even if we live in a simulation there's nothing we can do about it"[6]

---

[6] Are We Living in a Matrix SImulation?
https://youtu.be/Zz7K0TRFlo0

Science Proves Our Biology is a Storage Device

"I could collect all the movies ever made inside this tube.

... Before understanding how this is possible, it is important to understand the value of this achievement.

... Apart from the lack of space in our phones, we rarely think about our digital footprint.

... There is a non-profit website called the Internet Archive. In addition to free books and movies, there are web pages dating back to 1996. This is too exciting, and I went to take a look at the humble beginnings of the TED site. You can see that it has changed quite a bit over the past 30 years. So that led me to the very first TED in 1984, and it turned out to be a framework from Sony that explained how a compact disc works. (Laughs) It's amazing to be able to go back in time and access this moment. What's also fascinating is that 30 years after that first TED, we're still talking about digital storage.

And going back another 30 years, IBM launched the very first hard drive in 1956. It is seen here being loaded for delivery in front of a small audience. It contained the equivalent of an MP3 song and weighed over a ton.

At almost 9,000 euros per megabyte, I don't think anyone here would want to buy it, except maybe a collector. But it was the best we could do at the time. So much has been accomplished in terms of digital storage.

Devices have evolved enormously.

But these supports eventually wear out or become obsolete.

If someone gave you a floppy disk to save your presentation today, you'd laugh or give it a funny look, but you'd have no way to use it.

These media no longer meet our storage needs, although some of them can be converted. All technology eventually dies out or gets lost, along with our data, all our memories.

... Our data is our history, and even more so today. Our data will not be recorded on stone tablets. But we don't have to decide what matters now. There is a way to store everything. The solution happens to have been around for a few billion years, and it's in this tube. DNA is the oldest natural storage system. After all, it contains the information needed to build and preserve a human being.

What makes DNA so great? Take our own genome as an example. If we were to print the three billion A's, T's, C's and G's in one typeface, in a standard size, and stack all the sheets of paper, this pile would be about 130 meters high, between the Statue of Liberty and the Washington Monument.

Now, if we converted those A's, T's, C's and G's into numeric data, into zeros and ones, we'd get a few gigabytes. And this, in every cell of our body. We have over 30 trillion cells. You get the idea: DNA can store a ton of information in a tiny space. DNA is also very durable, and doesn't even need electricity to function. We know this because scientists have found DNA from humans who lived hundreds of thousands of years ago. One of them being Ötzi, the Iceman, who turns out to be Austrian. (Laughter) We found it well preserved, in the high mountains, between Italy and Austria, and it happens to have genetic relatives in Austria. One of you could be a cousin of Ötzi. (Laughter) The fact is that we have a better chance of recovering information from an ancestral human than from an old telephone.

... Storing data in DNA is not a new idea. Nature has been doing this for billions of years. In fact, every living being is a DNA storage medium. But how to store data in DNA? This is photo 51. This is the very first DNA photo, taken about 60 years ago. This is around the same time as IBM's hard drive. The knowledge of digital storage and that of DNA have evolved at the same time. We learned to sequence or read DNA, and quickly afterwards, to write or synthesize it. It is comparable to learning a new language. And now we can read, write and copy DNA. We do it all the time in the lab. So anything that can be stored as zeros and ones can be stored in DNA. To store something digitally, like this photo, we convert it to bits or binary digits. Each pixel in a black and white photo is simply a zero or a one. You can write DNA like a printer can print letters on a page. We just have to convert our data, all those zeros and ones, to A, T, C and G, and send it to a synthesis company. So we write, we save, and to recover our data, we sequence.

Now the fun part is deciding what kind of file to include. We are serious researchers; we therefore had to include a manuscript for future generations. We also included a 45 euro Amazon gift card -- no worries, the card is empty, someone decoded it

... Once we decided what kind of files to encode, we processed the data, converted the zeros and ones to A, T, C and G, and sent the file to a synthesis company. And this is what we were sent back [holds up tube of clear fluid]

All our files are in this tube. We just had to sequence them. It sounds simple enough, but the difference between a great idea and something you can actually use outweighs these practical challenges.

DNA may be stronger than any man-made device, but it's not perfect. He has his weaknesses. We recover the message by sequencing the DNA, and once the data is extracted, we lose the DNA. This is part of the sequencing process.

We don't want to run out of data, but luckily DNA can be copied, which is cheaper and easier than synthesizing it.   *[yeah def]*

We tried to make 200 trillion copies of our files, and we recovered all the data without error.

Sequencing also introduces errors into our DNA, in the A's, T's, C's and G's. Nature has a way of dealing with them in our cells. But our data is stored in synthetic DNA in a tube; so we had to find our own solution to solve this problem.

We therefore used an algorithm intended for streaming video. Watching a streaming video is basically trying to recover the original video, the original file. When we try to recover our original files, we simply do sequencing.

In reality, both processes consist of retrieving enough zeros and ones to restore our data. So, thanks to our coding strategy, we were able to process all our data in such a way that we could make billions of copies and recover all our files each time. Here's the movie we encoded. It's one of the first films ever made, and now the first to be copied more than 200 trillion times on DNA.

... Storage is not just the number of bytes, but our ability to store data and retrieve it. There has always been a tension between the volume of data that can be created, the volume that can be recovered and the volume that can be stored. Each advance in writing data demanded a new means of reading. Old media can no longer be read.

How many of you still have a CD drive in your computer, let alone a floppy disk?

This will never be the case with DNA. As long as we're alive, the DNA will be there, and we'll find a way to sequence it."[7]

---

[7] TED Talks. How can we store digital data in DNA | Dina Zielinski. https://youtu.be/wxStlzunxCw

Mathematics Proves What We See Is NOT Real

"Konnichiwa amigos! Today we have Donald Hoffman on the show ... Donald [is] a professor in the Department of Cognitive Sciences at the University of California Irvine if you guys haven't checked out his TED Talk ...

Donald: ...I think most of us just assume that, 'When i look at an apple and i see the red color and the apple shape and and so forth that ...you know ... i'm seeing the truth

... there really is an apple that exists and it would exist even if i weren't looking and you know we don't believe that we're seeing *all* of the truth but that we see those *aspects* of reality

that we need to survive and so and you know if i look up at the moon [that] we're seeing a reality

a genuine reality the shape ...the color... and so forth

[and] ... if we have a little bit of scientific background

maybe about evolution and so forth it an argument might be that you .. look ... you see the truth if you see reality as it is... in each generation ... probably you know were more more successful at feeding fighting fleeing and mating

(the big important actions of life)

and so they were more likely to pass on their genes that code for more accurate perceptions and and so you're based on that kind of intuitive logic it it makes sense that after you know thousands of generations of that we've been really shaped to see truths the truths that we need

.... most uh scientists mean who are actually experts in evolutionary theory [adhere to] an informal statement [or even] formally that evolution has shaped us to see reality as it is because that will make us more fit

... the idea is it's important for survival

....you know it it makes sense and you might go that's so obvious is you know why think about it any further it's just obviously true that you know we had to be shaped to see the truth

... of course no one thinks we see **all** of the truth, but those truths that we *need* [in terms of evolutionary advantage]

well so i decided ...14-15 years ago to really look at that carefully right and by that i mean   we all have an intuitive notion about evolution but it turns out that that intuition has been   turned into mathematics

... a guy named John Maynard Smith a British mathematician in the 1970s

used something called game theory ... the mathematics of game theory

... so i got a couple   graduate students who wanted to get their phds interested in this and they ran simulations [on evolution]

and the simulations suggested that organisms that saw reality as it IS could never ·

out compete organisms that saw **none** of reality   *[sooo, the exact opposite of what we intuitively believed to be true]*

.... I went to a mathematician Chaitan Prakash ... the bottom line is this it's a theorem of evolution by natural selection that the probability is precisely **zero**

that any structure that you perceive

whether it's the structure of shapes or colors any structure of your perceptions the probability of zero   that that structure that you perceive ... in any way represents a structure of objective reality,

... (whatever objective reality

is)

...So, it raises an obvious question right

... how in the world is... perception going to help us stay alive

if it's not showing us the truth about the world?

...It seems so counter-intuitive

... the answer ... is perhaps best understood by a metaphor

... there's a couple metaphors i think that are   helpful

one is if you're using a computer with a windows desktop ... and you have nice little   icons on your desktop ... you have this blue rectangular icon in the middle of your   desktop for ... an article that you're writing the article itself in your computer is not blue and rectangular and in the middle of the computer

even though the icon on your desktop is blue and rectangular in the middle of your desktop

and and   in that metaphor the reality is like all these voltages and magnetic fields and   you know circuits inside this computer that you may or may not even know about or you may have   no expertise in it and what you see is not circuits and software you just see eye candy

simple eye candy that lets you control all those circuits without even understanding them at all   right and and the point of the user interface is to let you control reality without even knowing   what the reality is most people have no idea about,

... digital circuits and ... how they work

... if you had to toggle voltages ... to write an email

no one would ever hear from you

...the point is that you can see that knowing the truth, being forced to deal with reality may **not** be a help

it could be a hindrance if i said the only way that you can send me an email is by toggling voltages well good luck it's not going to happen

but if i give you a nice simple user interface then it's easy and you don't have to know anything about reality and that's what evolution did what

these theorems are telling us is that the selection pressures from evolution are uniformly against forcing us to see the voltages and forcing us to toggle the voltages of reality whatever they might be instead is giving this a user interface with simple eye candy and ear candy and touch candy you know all of our senses are just user interfaces not the truth not so it's not just vision it's all senses and for all organisms not just humans this is a universal theorem for all sensory systems of all organisms we've all been shaped to have ... specific user interfaces that let us survive in our niche

so it's it's another metaphor would be... suppose someone says well i'm going to play [this video] game by toggling voltages in the supercomputer

well good luck i mean i'm going to be able to change lots of voltages in real time by just turning my steering wheel you're gonna have to toggle them   one at a time you have to know what you're doing too so so good luck

...even though you know the truth you're not gonna win the game and that's sort of what evolution has done is given us   the tools to win the game

lets us play the game of life and and win or or not

I   mean you know 99 [percent] of all species that have ever existed are extinct

so eventually we all lose

(we'll get back to that)

[...]
 the stuff i'm doing is fairly new so hopefully among cognitive scientists

[we will begin] to go beyond the headset

... it must open up a whole new realm now for young and upcoming scientists to really rethink a lot of the previous theories whether they will figure out the answer or not just to be able to rethink

... hopefully it'll get them... to rethink other things that perhaps were not questioned [in the past]

... it's like a person who ... has now become a pro at [a video game] but has no idea

about the circuits and software inside ... he doesn't have to be a computer programmer to   be a great player of the game and that's the point

being great players of the game of life   does not mean that we know what's going on in reality

... it's all virtual um and there are for those who who want some kind of help with that uh to understand   there's um phantom limb phenomena if you look at phantom limb so there are unfortunately people for   example have had an arm cut off um who still feel their arm they still feel like they have a hand   and they have they can phantom pains they can have phantom pains in their hand   and phantom experiences of cold hot itch pressure um and pain in and if you say where does it   hurt they'll point to empty space it hurts right there and there's nothing there and and so you're   actually constructing even your ex experience of touch is a virtual reality that that you construct   and this is true of of all of our senses

...

... as a scientist of course... i'm saying that there's a reality beyond space and time

... [but what is] objective reality?

That's what's happening to you   um so how do we answer that question? i think the   only way as a scientist for us to try to answer that question is to say look,

we can't answer it

until we propose a theory of objective reality beyond space and time

[...]

if people are are interested ...I published a paper called *Objects of Consciousness*

...just google   *Objects of Consciousness* and Hoffman you'll find the paper

...it's a   mathematically precise model of consciousness in which i try to boil down consciousness   to its bare bones

...that's what we do in science we try to come   up with the minimal assumptions that can boot up the entire field

...make as few assumptions as possible

So the assumptions i make about consciousness are that there are conscious experiences, [such as] smelling garlic, or having a headache

Raw, simple, conscious experiences

[these] may not [be] so simple

there are consciousnesses that that we can't even understand in fact most consciousness that we we can't even comprehend

…if i ask you imagine a specific color that you've never seen before can you can't right

i've asked a trivial little exercise of your imagination just imagine one stupid little color you've never seen before can't do it i'm saying that there's an infinite range or a countless range of possible experiences out there that other agents are having that you and i can't even concretely imagine that's how rich this this universe is

[....]

… there is interesting work um with near-death experiences um there was um a panel by the new york academy of sciences um last fall where they had a bunch of medical doctors in the new york area and elsewhere who who are dealing with people who have had no cortical activity for 20 30 40 minutes and they were able to resuscitate them   and these people do describe … similar experiences of a tunnel

a light

a life review

and all sorts of things

... i don't even know what i'm doing right now

when i pick up a cup with my hand... as a scientist, anymore

i literally don't know what i'm doing

my theory tells me i don't know what i'm

literally doing in reality

... you can begin to intelligently understand how you know the
steering   wheel and work and also in this case the example you get
how the brain works and how we might   interface with it

... we've got to reverse engineer the whole interface

...let me put another example

... so it's 1860 or something like that   and we've just discovered all these interesting things about electricity

... we don't know exactly how it works and there's no technology yet

But... we realized that

... somehow electricity can do stuff
miraculously
across space and time

and so we think okay so this   is the mystical thing what is this the mystical thing that can connect us and maybe if we like   have seances and hold hands we can use this power to actually communicate with people on the other   side of the world using electricity

well it turns out you're right that you can use electricity to communicate with people on the other side of the world but it's going to take you a century   of hard work and mathematical modeling to allow

what you and i are doing right now - i'm in direct   contact with you

you're in spain

i'm in california

we're literally on opposite

sides of the world

we're using electricity to do

what would seem miraculous

to people in 1840 1850

but we didn't get there by holding hands

... we got there through hard mathematical analysis

years and years of technology development

development of infrastructure

and ... that's my guess is what what's going to happen here

... i mean you just can't leap there

from here

we've got all this mathematical modeling to do

we have to   understand the network of conscious agents

how it works

understand really what happens at death

In this relationship to the interface

... i mean there are scientists that are claiming that you know
there are black holes that exist in the universe if you were to pass
it there are millions of other universes that could exist

... well um the thing about black holes is um

the best theory that we have of them right now

tells us there's a **singularity** at the center

when you go through across the event horizon of a black hole
space and time reverse rolls the arrow inward is now time and
the arrow points you to the singularity

what's really happening is that you're being
sucked into a singularity where you're destroyed
so how how you might there you might be able to
open up wormholes ... into other realms

...black hole science is ... much more sophisticated than it was
you know 100 years ago

but we don't even really know what happens

... so i'm not really proposing

... i'm [just] saying that there **may** be

... just like, your body

which is my icon right

[but somehow]

i've got a portal

to your consciousness

... i can affect how you feel

i can affect how you think

it's truly a remarkable [idea that by] using these portals we can go back and forth these   are not black holes these are just portals

that we use in our interface that affect consciousnesses

[...]

... we're taking our first step out of the headset

... scientists should be really grateful we've just... opened up a whole new vista

we're taking the first step out of the headset

... if you want to go   into this, by the way, learn mathematics ... physics and neuroscience ... and computer science ...   serious mathematics ... information theory... this is no nonsense hard hard work ahead

[end]"[8]

[8] Sean Kim, Donald Hoffman Proves That We Live in a Simulation. https://youtu.be/iAfjsktMXu8

How to Design Your Life and Exist the Matrix & more from Dr. Donald Hoffman

"Our best science tells us that space-time is not fundamental

... the new Nobel Prize this year ... is insane [it] literally just says you're in a simulation

and it's the same as rendering and when you look at something it renders

when you look away it it doesn't and we can prove it mathematically

[...]

... we're doing some science
we're talking
we're learning to love each other
which maybe you know who knows that might be the big thing
maybe maybe it's learning to know yourself
beyond any concepts

and to know that everybody else is really you under a different Avatar and to to learn to love I mean I I don't know what the final answer is but this is the kind of question that comes up and the kind of answer that comes up

.... why would why would Consciousness, this Grand Consciousness,

that the math seems to point to

why would it need to understand itself why would it need to discover love?

... In some sense ... we have to learn to live with [saying], 'I'm not going to get the final Theory of Everything'

no matter even if you're an Einstein...

I'm saying we need a theory of Consciousness outside space-time because our best science tells us that space-time is a trivial data structure

it's a shallow trivial data structure

why should we try to shoehorn Consciousness to be something inside space-time why not think about again the VR case with my headset all that I'm perceiving is actually not really there it's actually in my Consciousness let's turn things around space-time and particles in the physical world is just a little tiny data structure inside consciousness

... science has been inside the headset until the last couple decades all of our science has been studying the pixels in our headset and the structure of our pixel

... [now] science is taking a step outside the headset and saying what is beyond space and time?

so that's really incredible

... the essential thing is the the awareness and the the real Joy of being is the awareness itself

... there is no Theory of Everything but that doesn't mean that we should just do whatever we wish and think what random thoughts we want, No.

... We're rewarded by thinking precisely and also humbly

[First] precisely to get as far as our current framework will go, and then humbly to realize that it's just a framework **and there's a new one beyond**

... and that will also be rigorous so ...it's not going into you know just whatever you want

... I'll put it this way ... some people [think that since we have proof that life is a simulation, none of this is real, that therefore it's ok to] do whatever you want ... I think that that's just plain wrong ... because it tells the limits of itself"[9] [meaning, you could do whatever you want, but then you will never be able to uncover the wonderful surprises and blessings that are befallen onto those who open themselves up to the idea. You'd be limited to your own ideas.]

[9] Tim Bilyeu, REALITY IS AN ILLUSION: How To Design Your Dream Life & EXIT THE MATRIX | Donald Hoffman. https://youtu.be/RIRHq3d7Uuo

Science Proves You Don't Exist

"You don't exist, and science is pretty confident of that fact. Well, it would be unfair to say that you don't exist, you probably do. Just not in the way that   you think you do.

Instead of flesh and body, you're likely nothing more than electrons on a   circuit board, your consciousness a long string of code being run by a supercomputer somewhere.

You believe you're real because you've been programmed to think you're real- or perhaps,   if you're really lucky, you actually are real, and it's the rest of the world that's fake.

But wait,   let's back up a second because we can already feel some of our audience's heads spinning.

Simulation theory is exactly what it sounds like: our universe, and perhaps our very selves,   is nothing more than a simulation

… You might be tempted to turn to computer engineers for an answer to the simulation theory question,   but it turns out that spiritual gurus may have a better grip on the ultimate   answer than a scientist or engineer.

After all, spiritual gurus dedicate themselves to the study and development of the spiritual side of life, seeking to understand the fundamental question of why do we exist at all?

The problem with turning to scientists for an answer on simulation theory is simply put, that any evidence they can discover to disprove the theory could itself be simulated.

Perhaps religion and spiritualism can give us a better perspective on the question if we are real or not, and religion has some very uncomfortable clues that we might in fact be simulated.

Eastern religions have a staggering amount of evidence supporting that we in fact live in a   simulation.

One of the Buddha's most well known teachings is as follows:

All phenomena are like reflections appearing in a very clear mirror,   devoid of inherent existence.

In essence, this perfectly describes any video game- everything you see in a video game may look real, and have a real effect on a character inside the video game,   but it is all ultimately not real to any observer outside of the video game itself.

If you log into Fortnite and someone shoots directly at you, the real you behind the screen is completely unharmed by the digital bullets being shot in your direction.

Even more disturbing is the ultimate goal of Buddhism- Nirvana.

Nirvana is the ultimate spiritual goal of a Buddhist practitioner, and only achieved by rising above the "three poisons", greed, aversion, and ignorance.

Once you accomplish that task, you are rewarded by being freed from the constant cycle of rebirth, where you live and die a series of lives meant to act as teaching experiences.

Achieving nirvana leads to parinirvana, or the final nirvana, an afterlife for souls that have been freed from the Hindu and Buddhist cycle of rebirth.

What happens here is indescribable, and the human brain cannot understand it so there is nothing known about it.

At a glance, Buddhism's nirvana seems much like the carrot-and-stick core ideology of any religion- do good and be rewarded with good, do bad and get the stick by being forced to live yet another life in our imperfect world. Yet for a computer gamer, the entire concept of nirvana has a disturbingly 'quest-like' feature reminiscent of any computer game.

It even comes with a respawn feature, just like you would respawn in a game over and over again until you succeed by overcoming the obstacle in front of you. Imagine a game of Super Mario, with Mario respawning over and over in front of the bottomless pit he can't quite get the hang of jumping over- until he does one day and continues on his way.

Buddhism's nirvana seems to point at one of several possibilities for why we even live in a simulation, which we'll get to soon- but first, what do other religions say?

In the Hindu tradition life is believed to be nothing more than a dream of Vishnu, and every single human being, along with all of their history, triumphs, and defeats, nothing more than a miniscule portion of the fabric making up that dream.

When Vishnu awakens, we will cease to exist, no different than if we were being simulated by a computer and the simulation ended, or the computer shut off. Christianity, Judaism, and Islam, whom all share the same God, don't have as obvious links to the possibility of the universe being simulated, but they do share a belief in a monotheistic God who created us to have a personal relationship with him directly.

The concept of a single God in control of the entire universe is no different than the concept of a super intelligent AI creating a simulated universe, and then populating it with simulated life.

Religion, especially eastern religion, seems to have strong links to simulation hypothesis, but what does science say?

Well, the most important thing to remember is that if our simulators wished to hide the fact that we were living in a simulation from us, then we would never be able to find out as any evidence proving it could be simply edited, and any evidence disproving it could be itself simulated.

Think back on the last time you played a single player video game and engaged in the questionable behavior of 'save scumming', or reloading a previous save so you could get a beneficial, or the best, outcome.

Your character has in effect witnessed the effects of any number of possible outcomes, but you literally reversed time for that character and he or she is now only aware of one outcome- the one you chose for it. So too might our simulators simply reload a previous save state and then steer us away from the earth shattering discovery that we are in fact, simulations.

But if everything can be edited and we can't even trust our own observations or deductions, can there ever be any evidence that we live in a simulation?

Well, yes, possibly.

One piece of evidence, and it's definitely not good if you like to think you are a real flesh and blood person, comes from simple probability.

We have observed our own universe and deduced that it largely makes sense.

Sure, there's some things that still bother scientists, but by and large, the universe seems to be understandable, and the processes by which it operates are themselves also understandable.

That would seem to indicate then that there is a greater probability that our simulated universe is a very close approximation of the real universe.

After all, you're more likely to create a simulation using values for the universe that you already know work- never underestimate the probabilistic power of complacency driving people to the path of least resistance.

This means that the real universe is likely as large as ours, which in turn means that it could potentially be inhabited by numerous highly advanced species- yet no matter how many real, unsimulated beings inhabited the real universe, the ability to condense information onto a computer means that by sheer numbers alone, the number of simulated minds are inevitably exponentially greater than non-simulated minds.

That gives you pretty crap odds of being real. But this is a rather imperfect argument, as it relies on a number of values that we simply can't ever have precise data on.

The real universe might in fact be tiny compared to our simulated universe- our vast, seemingly infinite universe could be nothing more than a fantasy dreamt up by a super intelligent species stuck in a boring, mundane universe that's no bigger than a few solar systems.

Consider the popularity of movies, books, and video games set in exciting worlds that are vastly different than our boring, mundane earth.

Intelligence seems to yearn for novelty, and is easily bored by its own everyday reality- so the real argument here might be that if our universe is simulated, then the real universe is far more mundane than ours.

Physics might offer better clues to the true nature of our universe.

In a computer simulation, what you can see is limited by the resolution of the program, and if you look close enough you discover the individual pixels that make up each image.

In our world, atoms share very similar properties with pixels, as we know that atoms make up everything in our material world.

Yet, atoms themselves are made up of even smaller particles known as elementary particles such as gluons and quarks, with the latter being the smallest particle we know of.

If our universe is simulated, then why add unnecessary complexity by increasing the resolution of our simulation down to the level of quarks?

Why not change the fundamentals of radioactive decay so that particles smaller than atoms- which we believed for a long time were the building blocks of all existence- didn't need up quarks and down quarks to operate? It seems like adding even smaller fundamental particles is simply adding complexity, and in a simulation this means added computational power that seems to be completely unnecessary.

Unless our simulators exist in a universe with unlimited energy, it's extremely dubious that they would run simulations requiring so much energy input to power the massive amounts of computation needed to simulate every single quark in our fake universe.

Then there's the consideration of the massive amounts of waste heat generated by the supercomputers crunching such incredible amounts of numbers to make our universe work.

It's famously said that in order to be able to simulate the entire universe- every single particle within it- you would need a computer as big, or bigger than the universe, which also seems to indicate that simulation theory is dead on arrival.

Yet modern video games offer clues to getting around this huge problem. When you play a video game, your computer only animates the part of the world you are currently looking at.

After all, there's no sense in wasting the computing power to animate whatever is going on behind you.

Instead, those details are stripped down to the most bare amounts of information needed to keep tabs on the parts of the world you aren't looking at, and when you move the camera around the computer then simulates the new viewpoint complete with graphical representations for what was just seconds ago, nothing more than data.

You've all experienced what happens when a video game isn't coded optimally to do this, or when your computer is getting old and slow, and games you play stutter or hang often as the computer struggles to turn data into graphical representations.

So if our universe is simulated, one way to get around having to constantly track every single molecule, atom, and quark in existence, is to simply not load those objects until needed- like when scientists start cracking atoms open to discover what lies inside of them.

Not only would a simulation rarely need to devote the computing power to simulate atoms or quarks, because we are after all rarely ever interacting with them in a direct way, but it could completely ignore these elements when they aren't necessary.

Until the invention of the microscope, our simulation would have had no need to simulate every single individual cell, bacteria, or virus, as we were completely oblivious to their existence and had no way of detecting them.

Right now our simulation doesn't need to simulate the weather systems of every single planet in the universe, it only needs to run localized simulations in the very, very small areas of our own solar system we've explored, like a few dozen miles around our Mars rovers for example.

In essence, it's the classic question of does a tree falling in a forest make any noise if nobody is around to hear it- only in this case the tree makes no noise, and doesn't even fall, because there's no need to waste computer power simulating any of that if nobody is around to hear or see it."[10]

---

[10] The Infographics Show. Science Proves You Don't Exist
https://youtu.be/EgxK-72LK8Q

Conclusion

If indeed we are living in a simulation, what does this mean? Many people interpret this as proof of a Higher Power, otherwise known as Inspired Design, or Creationism:

"... the idea that 'we' are separate from 'them', that 'they' are separate from 'us',

... It's this incredible sense that we're not safe.

And the truth is that we **are** safe.

We are already safe.

We are already ONE,

we don't have to...   'get' anywhere.

We are *already* there,

wherever **there** is!

... What is the lesson of this? ... as a human being, I'll avoid discomfort, like the plague. Human beings don't like to be uncomfortable.

... But you know, being uncomfortable doesn't mean we're not safe.

... I always use the analogy of going to the gym

you're not **comfortable** lifting the weight [or being in a physical reality with challenges and limitations] but you have to break down the muscle

... it's not comfortable for lifting weights.

...I'd rather be at home, eating, you know, eating anything and watching Netflix. It's a much more comfortable place to be yes, yes, yes.

But you don't grow and exercise muscles and things like that.

And then other problems ensue.

So living in a comfort zone is not a very good thing.

... the tiger around the corner, that guy might eat you.

... now it's not literal tigers .... It's everything else in the world that we do, whether it's your own personal challenges that you want to deal with and things like that.

It's pretty fascinating. It's quite fascinating."[11]

"... Some people don't like the idea of the simulated world because it assumes that we are just a bunch of programmable beings without free will

... if we are in a simulation then what is to say that the programmer wouldn't have already programmed [into our experience] that there is no way to tell it's a simulation

[or, since, we already figured out it IS a simulation... i mean right what just happened I thought we just went over this in great detail!?

.. ok, so anyway.. Then what is to say that the 'programmer wouldn't have already programmed into our experience the concept of Free Will? In the same way that light has been proven to be both a light and a particle, could we not somehow- in a way that is admittedly well beyond our human level of conscious understanding- live in a world with the existence of both free will and the 'program'?]

many scientists view [a theory of Simulated existence] to be unprovable

---

[11] Next Level Soul Podcast https://youtu.be/Y4dU9nu8xQQ

in any concrete sense … any evidence that is directly observed could be another simulation itself *[true, yes]*

… Even if we are a simulated reality, there is no way to be sure." *[and]* [12]

---

[12] Science Time. The Simulation Hypothesis and Free WIll.
https://youtu.be/LMneQsUw6XI

Footnotes

1. "We're in the Matrix" Tech CEO's Cryptic Last Words. https://youtu.be/oMmoMZzsAVE

2. Why Files. https://youtu.be/4wMhXxZ1zNM

3. Dr. Incognito. The Simulation Hypothesis Documentary. https://youtu.be/pznWo8fo2oI

4. Fexl, The Universe is Not Real- And Nothing Actually Exists. https://youtu.be/GQpgVWLqo_c

5. Hidden Halo, James Gates Shocks Neil DeGrasse Tyson We Live In A Computer Simulation https://www.youtube.com/watch?v=KSe3rRizzFE

6. Are We Living in a Matrix SImulation? https://youtu.be/Zz7KoTRFloo

7. TED Talks. How can we store digital data in DNA | Dina Zielinski. https://youtu.be/wxStlzunxCw

8. Sean Kim, Donald Hoffman Proves That We Live in a Simulation. https://youtu.be/iAfjsktMXu8

9. Tim Bilyeu, REALITY IS AN ILLUSION: How To Design Your Dream Life & EXIT THE MATRIX | Donald Hoffman. https://youtu.be/RIRHq3d7Uuo

10. The Infographics Show. Science Proves You Don't Exist https://youtu.be/EgxK-72LK8Q

11. Next Level Soul Podcast https://youtu.be/Y4dU9nu8xQQ

12. Science Time. The Simulation Hypothesis and Free WIll. https://youtu.be/LMneQsUw6XI